# MAKE NO PROVISION for the FLESH

Evelyn W. Miller, Ph.D

WESTBOW°
PRESS
A DIVISION OF THOMAS NELSON
& ZONDERVAN

Unless otherwise noted, the bible versions used in this publication are the:
The New Spirit Filled Life Bible
Copyright 1982 by Thomas Nelson, Inc

The Amplified Bible
Copyright 1965 by Zondervan Publishing House

The Message
Copyright 1993 by Eugene H. Peterson

Unless otherwise noted, the definitions used in this publication are from the:
Vine's Complete Expository Dictionary of Old and New Testament Words
Copyright 1985 by Thomas Nelson, Inc Publishers

WestBow Press books may be ordered through booksellers or by contacting:

WestBow Press
A Division of Thomas Nelson & Zondervan
1663 Liberty Drive
Bloomington, IN 47403
www.westbowpress.com
1 (866) 928-1240

ISBN: 978-1-4908-6766-3 (sc)
ISBN: 978-1-4908-6767-0 (e)

Library of Congress Control Number: 2015901132

Print information available on the last page.

WestBow Press rev. date: 3/3/2015

# FOREWORD

I have had the privilege of serving God for 44 years and have been an ordained minister for 40 years with the Association of International Gospel Assemblies, Inc. I served on the International Board of Ministers of our association as well as the state chairman of Texas.

We pioneered and pastured an interdenominational church for 15 years during which time we supported and established churches, orphanages, and a bible school in Mexico. Under the direction of the Holy Spirit, I was able to establish an aviation ministry, Missions Airlift, introducing churches in Missouri, Arkansas, Oklahoma and Texas to Mission work in Mexico.

At the present time, my wife and I are pastors of the Bridge Builders, ages 55 and older, of New Life Worship Center in Tyler, Texas.

Evelyn Miller makes it clear the church is losing its' focus from the Lord to the world and has lost the desire for the Word of God. She has a desire to see a fresh move of the Holy Spirit upon God's people creating a hunger for Him and His word. She encourages us to examine the scriptures for ourselves to cleanse ourselves of all those things that are contrary to living a holy life as God requires us to live. This is only possible by reading the Word of God through the power of the Holy Spirit. We see the problem of the church in this day and time but there is hope and it is God's will that we know Him and live for Him. This can be done by faith.

Bill Orr
Bridge Builder's Pastor
New Life Worship Center
Tyler, Texas 75703

# CONTENTS

# INTRODUCTION

*T*he picture of the church today is very disturbing to me. The people of God are being attacked with illnesses. Cancer, diabetes, high blood pressure, and arthritis are attacking the body.

I also see the church become a revolving door. People would come in accept Christ, remain for a while and leave. Along with this, ministries are failing.

The people of God are living in bondage. Jesus said he came that we might have life more abundantly. It is evident that we are living below our privileges. We do not understand that the abundant life means more than having material things. If we seek first, the kingdom of God and its righteousness, those things will be added to us. The necessities of life are provided and other things will be added. He also says if we delight ourselves in the Lord he will give us the desires of our heart.

Psalms 37:4: "Delight yourself in the Lord, and He shall give you the desire of your heart."

No one desires sickness, disease, poverty and worry.

We are living in the hour that the church needs to move aggressively and take the kingdom by force. The Kingdom of heaven is set up by Jesus Christ. It is a powerful reign among us. The Kingdom of God is to be understood by spiritual means. The kingdom of God is to be entered into by spiritual means and in practical living. It requires a strong and radical reaction by believers. We are to enter the kingdom of God by intense determination and be bold about serving Christ. We are to be committed and willing with enthusiasm to respond and take the message of Christ into the world. The message of Christ must be in us first. We are to be the first partakers of this gospel.

We need to maintain a state of readiness for battle. We lose our battle stance by letting the word of God we have heard slip.

Hebrews 2:1: "Therefore we must give the more earnest heed to the things we have heard, lest we drift away."

When we let the word of God slip from us, we drift away into opposing doctrines; which moves us away from our convictions. Our spirit man becomes weak and the flesh becomes strong. We begin to make provisions to fulfill the lust of our flesh.

Romans 13:14 says "But put ye on the Lord Jesus Christ and make no provision for the flesh, to fulfill its lust;"

We put on the Lord Jesus Christ by:
1. Submitting to His word; that is, agreeing with His word for our lives.
2. Living in fellowship with Him.
3. Depending on Him and His Strength.

We should do nothing to nurture the flesh's sensual appetites and desires.

Jesus took away all of our sins upon Himself on the cross. He took stripes, whippings on His back for our healing.

1 Peter 2:24 "Who his own self bare our sins in his own body on the tree, that we being dead to sins, should live unto righteousness; by whose stripes ye were healed."

The body of Christ is going through many attacks of the enemy in our families, bodies, finances, marriages, and everything that concerns living in the earth. The word of God says that we will have trials and tribulations but He will deliver us out of them all. And as Christ told Paul, His grace is sufficient for him. His grace is sufficient for us as well.

Christ over came the world. He has given us what we need to overcome the world also – His word.

Many times we make provision for the lusts of the flesh without realizing what we are doing. It could be that we are in a state of a lack of knowledge in this area of our lives.

I began to seek God. As I cried out to God I kept hearing him say make no provision for the flesh. I began a journey in the study of how we make provisions for the flesh.

This book is written to provide information in this area of our Christian journey and bring awareness to how we open doors to the enemy ourselves.

It is my prayer that Holy Spirit will bring deliverance as we meditate on the word of God and make changes in our lives. The Grace of God is here to help us in our daily walk. God's mercies are renewed every day. We can be victorious in this life.

# THE FLESH

We must first understand us, the human, being born with a sinful nature. If we are Body, soul and spirit, then what is "flesh?"

We use the word flesh all of the time. Preachers, teachers, all who minister the word of God teach or refer to the "flesh".

But what are the hearers thinking when we say "the flesh?" I believe there needs to be a deeper understanding of the "flesh."

Basar is the Hebrew word for flesh. It means the "meaty part plus the skin" of men. The first occurrence is in Genesis 2:21 when God took one of Adam's ribs and closed up the flesh.

Genesis 2:21 "And the Lord caused a deep sleep to fall on Adam, and he slept; and he took one of his ribs, and closed up the flesh instead thereof;"

The word can also be applied to the "meaty part" of animals. Basar represents edible animal "flesh" or "meat" cooked or uncooked. It can also refer to "meat" that is forbidden to eat.

Exodus 21:28 "If an ox gore a man or a woman, that they die; then the ox shall be surely stoned, and his flesh shall not be eaten; but the owner of the ox shall be quilt."

Flesh sometimes means blood relative.

Genesis 29:14 "And Laban said unto Jacob, surely thou art my bone and my flesh, and he abode with him the space of a month."

About 50 times, "flesh" represents the "physical aspect" of man or animal as contrast with the spirit, soul, or heart (the nonphysical aspect).

Sarx in the Hebrew has a wider range of meaning in the New Testament than the Old Testament.

In this instance "flesh" can mean the substance of the body; the human body; and the weaker element in human nature, the unregenerate state of men.

Flesh can mean the seat of sin in man. This is not referring to the physical body.

2 Peter 2:18, "For when they speak great swelling words of emptiness, they allure through the lusts of the flesh, through lewdness, the ones who have actually escaped from those who live in error."

The speakers are false teachers alluring those who have let the word slip through the lust of the flesh.

1 John 2:16, "For all that is in the world-the lust of the flesh, the lust of the eyes, and the pride of life- is not of the Father but is of the world."

Flesh can be referred to the lower and temporary element in the Christian.

Galatians 3:3, "Are you so foolish? Having begun in the spirit, are you now being made perfect by the flesh?"

Galatians 6:8, "For he who sows to his flesh will of the flesh reap corruption, but he who sows to the spirit will of the spirit reap everlasting life."

Paul uses sowing and reaping to moral behavior. Sow only what you want to reap. God will surely bring the harvest.

The flesh is the carnal that denotes the sinful element in man's nature, by reason of decent from Adam. The spiritual is that which comes by the regenerating operation of the Holy Spirit.

The flesh that we are dealing with is more than the meat on our bones. It is that sinful nature. The meat on our bones can do nothing of its self.

If the sinful nature rules the mind; the mind tell the body what to do, and the body obeys, we can then walk in sin.

If the Holy Spirit has regenerated the spirit and the regenerated spirit rules the mind; the mind can tell the body what the spirit says to do, and we obey it, then we can walk in the spirit. If Christians are to obey Romans 13:14, we must know what is the lusts of the flesh. In dealing with our flesh we must deal with lust.

Romans 13:14 "But put ye on the Lord Jesus Christ, and make not provision for the flesh, to fulfill the lusts thereof."

# CONSIDER THESE TRUTHS

Jesus is coming back for a church without spot or wrinkle. When Jesus comes He wants to find His people clean inside and out.

All Flesh is not the same but there is one kind of flesh of mankind. We are to love ourselves.

We should not take our holiness for granted. We should protect our holiness. We protect it by continuing to turn away from sin. We must break away from our past life and give ourselves to God alone.

The life, which we now live in the flesh, we live by the faith of the Son of God. We must realize that we cannot live this life with out Christ. The flesh will not permit it.

We have not received the spirit of God by the flesh. We are not being made perfect by the flesh or by obeying the traditions of men. We receive the Holy Spirit by faith. We grow by the work that God does in us and our faith in Christ. Sowing and reaping is a law of life. If you sow to the flesh you will reap to the flesh.

# PROVISION

*P*rovision, pronoia, means to know ahead of time.

It is fore planning, foresight, forethought, premeditated plan, making preparation for, and providing for.

It is derived from pro, "before," and noeo, "to think," "contemplate."Provision means providence, care, and prudence.

When our mind is constantly on providing for what the flesh wants rather than what God says, we are always preparing for gratifying the flesh.

We will work two jobs and neglect the commandments of God, our children and families.

We will not have time to pray, read our bibles, (which is how we get to know about God, who we are, what God thinks about us, His promises), and etc., attend church which we are called to do in fellowship with other believers, or serve others in visiting the sick, those in prison, feeding the hungry, clothing the naked and praying for one another.

## CONSIDER THESE TRUTHS

We are to owe no man but to love man. Christ loved us so much he died for us. We can only love one another as Christ loves us. We should owe no man love.

We are humans and we are weak. But in Christ we are made strong. Therefore we are to use Christ's strength to win our battles. We are to use God's battle plans for our life. He has provided spiritual weapons for us to use. We must remember that God is spirit.

We make provisions for the flesh in many ways without realizing that is what we are doing. It is all rooted in the lust of the eyes, the lust of the flesh, and the pride of life.

Lust and pride are designed to produce sin in our lives. The Bible gives us warnings, examples, and solutions for those temptations. We can overcome them. We must not provide for them in our lives. We are instructed to watch and pray because we are influenced by what our eyes see, our ears hear, our hands touch, our mouth speaks and places we go.

# PLACE

*T*he Greek word for place (Topos) emphasizes that believers can actually give ground in their lives to satanic control.

Speaking words that are contrary to God's words can give place to the enemy.

When this happens, the enemy will bring thoughts to your mind that is contrary to the word of God. If the thoughts are entertained long enough you will act on them; Thus causing problems in your circumstances that bring no good resolution.

## CONSIDER THESE TRUTHS

Romans 12:19: "Dearly beloved, avenge not yourselves, but rather give place unto wrath: for it is written, vengeance is mine; I will repay, saith the Lord."

Satan can take advantage of us when we don't obey, submit, or agree with God's word. We are to forgive not try to get revenge.

Satan walks around as a roaring lion. We are to submit to God and resist him. Be steadfast in the faith knowing that we all go through trials.

1 Peter 5:8-9 "Be sober, be vigilant; because your adversary the devil walks about like a roaring lion seeking whom he may devour; resist him, steadfast in the faith, knowing that the same afflictions are accomplished in your brethren that are in the world."

Ephesians 6:13 tells us to put on the whole armor of God that we may be able to withstand in the evil day... Withstand in the Greek is Anthistemi. Anti-against and histemi-to cause to stand.

Ephesians 6:13 "Wherefore take unto you the whole armour of God, that you may be able to withstand in the evil day, and having done all, to stand."

We can stand face to face against an adversary; we can stand our ground with the authority and spiritual weapons given to us by God.

More Scriptures:  Psalm 4:4; 37:8
2 Corinthians 2:10-11
James 4:7

The enemy does not have any new methods of attack. He uses the same methods with new strategies.

1 John 2:16 says, "For all that is in the world, the lust of the flesh, and the lust of the eyes, and the pride of life, is not of the Father, but of the world."

Satan is the prince of this world. We will take a brief look at each of Satan's methods.

# THE WORKS OF
# THE FLESH

## LUST OF THE FLESH

Galatians 5:19-20 records the works of the flesh. They manifest, appear, and are apparent. The flesh is the principle that moves men to commit these works. These are sins that will shut men out of heaven.

If we are Christ's, we must make it our constant care to crucify the flesh. We must not yield ourselves as servants of sin. Christ will never own us if we yield ourselves as servants of sin. We must sincerely endeavor to die to sin.

As we cease to do evil we must learn to do well. We must oppose the works of the flesh and bring forth the fruit of the Spirit.

The sinful nature tells a person to lust. That is why there is conflict between the spirit and the flesh.

Galatians 5:16-17, "I say then: walk in the Spirit, and you shall not fulfill the lust of the flesh. For the flesh lusts against the Spirit and the Spirit against the flesh; and these are contrary to one another, so that you do not do the things that you wish."

A Christian should walk in the spirit in order to not fulfill the lust of the flesh. The flesh lust against the spirit and the spirit lusted against the flesh. They are contrary to one another. This is why Christians have a hard time doing the right things in life.

Lust is the active and individual desire resulting from indulging in things that dishonor us, wound us, and hurt us. It is the diseased condition of the soul.

Lust operates on impulse. Lust always reaches out after and toward something with the purpose of satisfying self and drawing to one's self.

The works of the flesh are adultery, fornication, uncleanness, lasciviousness, idolatry, witchcraft, hatred, variance, emulations, wrath, strife, seditions, heresies, envying, murders, drunkenness, reveling and anything like these.

# SINS OF LUST

## ADULTERY

Adultery is of a Judeo-Christian origin. It is common to Judaism, Christianity, and Islam and applies particularly to women.

In the Old Testament times, females were first owned by their parents then their husbands. They were taken as a wife by sex, money, or deed; thus becoming property of the husband.

A man committed adultery when he went in unto a woman sexually if she was married or had been married.

It is voluntary sexual intercourse between a married person and partner other than the lawful husband or wife.

Adultery is the willful and harmful violation of the primary, the permanence, and the honesty of the marriage.

Adultery often begins because of needs not being met in the marriage. It destroys marriages and families. Some examples that demonstrate adultery are:

Day and night time soap operas

The movie industry

Pornography

Lustful novels

They present acts of adultery as entertaining also including the damages done to families. It is not interpreted as being real only entertainment.

To love and submit to each other as the scriptures commands is a weapon against adultery.

Understanding covenant is a weapon of knowledge against adultery.

This is why the Pharisees used the woman that was caught in the act of adultery to try and trap Jesus and Jesus could give the statement, "You who is without sin cast the first stone."

Jesus' fulfillment of the law caused the true meanings of the scriptures to come to light.

Jesus included in His teaching that whosoever looketh on a woman to lust after her hath committed adultery with her already in his heart.

Matthew 5:28 "But I say unto you, that whosoever looketh on a woman to lust after her hath committeth adultery with her already in his heart."

We must not forget about spiritual adultery. When we are saved we are lawfully married to Jesus Christ. When we go after other gods we are committing adultery. We can play the harlot as Israel and Judah did.

Jeremiah 3:6 "The Lord said also unto me in the days of Josiah the king, hast thou seen that which backsliding Israel hath done? She is gone up upon every high mountain and under every green tree, and there hath played the harlot."

Jeremiah 3:8 "And I saw when for all the causes whereby backsliding Israel committed adultery I had put her away, and given her a bill of divorce; yet her treacherous sister Judah feared not, but went and played the harlot also."

If we commit adultery against God we will be cast into great tribulation unless we repent.

Revelation 2:22 "Behold, I will cast her into a bed, and them that commit adultery with her into great tribulation, except they repent of their deeds."

The apostate church (church turned from God) is an adulteress.

## FORNICATION

Fornication is sexual relationship between the unmarried. It produces immorality which reduces personal value.

Proverbs 6:25-26 "Lust not after her beauty in thine heart; neither let her take thee with her eyelids. For by means of a whorish woman a man is brought to a piece of bread: and the adulteress will hunt for the precious life."

While fornication is not limited to teens and young adults, it is in high rate among them. They develop their own codes. One being oral sex does not constitute intercourse.

Living together before marriage is also rated high in this era.

In an article entitled "Almost Everyone's Doing It" from Relevant Magazine, a poll showed 80% of Evangelical singles admitted to having pre-marital sex.

The media contributes to the dictates of the flesh through the lust of the eyes. The things we watch can elicit and/or call forth sexual intercourse.

The association of pagan idolatry and doctrines when one has confessed adherence to the Christian faith can be considered fornication.

The punishment of Sodom and Gomorrha is a paradigm of God's judgment against immorality.

Jude 7 "Even as Sodom and Gomorrah, and cities about them in like manner, giving themselves over to fornication, and going after strange flesh, are set forth for an example, suffering the vengeance of eternal fire."

## UNCLEANNESS

Uncleanness is contamination by ritual, physical, moral, or spiritual impurity. Uncleanness is the clothing of those engaged in immorality.

Jude 23 "And others save with fear, pulling them out of the fire; hating even the garment spotted by the flesh."

Unnatural pollutions whether acted out by ones self or another is uncleanness.

## LASCIVIOUSNESS

Lasciviousness is unbridled lust, wantonness and readiness for all pleasure. It acknowledges no restraint. It is riotous excess. It is overt, open and observable, perversion.

We have given names to these acts in order to authenticate them. Making the acts a style of how one lives. Such as married couples being "swingers."

Romans 1:26-27 "For this cause God gave them up unto vile affections; for even their women did change the natural use into that which is against nature; And likewise also the men, leaving the natural use of the woman, burned in their lust one toward another: men with men working that which is unseemly, and receiving in themselves that recompense, penalty, of their error which was meet."

# SINS OF IMPIETY AND SUPERSTITION

## IDOLATRY

Worship of false gods - idols. It is the desires of the power of the evil lurking, lying in wait, in your members; those animal impulses and all that is earthy in you that is employed sin; sexual vices, impurity, sensual appetites, unholy desires, all greed and covetousness. The worship of idols is the worship of demons.

We must also understand that we have the capacity to make idols. Anything we love and worship before God can be an idol to us.

1 Corinthians 10:20 "But I say, that the things which the Gentiles sacrifice, they sacrifice to devils, and not

to God; and I would not that you should have fellowship with devils."

# WITCHCRAFT

The use of drugs, whether simple or potent, was generally accompanied by incantations, speaking words and or slogans repeatedly to produce some kind of effect; and appeals to occult, secret or hidden powers; with the provision of various charms, amulets, etc., professedly designed to keep the applicant or patient from the attention and power of demons, but actually to impress the applicant or patient with the mysterious resources and powers of the sorcerer.

It is the practice of sorcery. Controlling others is the main purpose of witchcraft. Whatever method used to control others is as the sin of witchcraft.

God created man with free will. This should never be taken away when a person is of a well mind. We must reject spiritual counsel from any source that does not speak according to the word of God.

Unholy methodology leads to unholy alliances. We are to serve God and God alone.

Isaiah 8:19 "And when they shall say unto you, seek unto them that have familiar spirits and unto wizards that peep and that mutter: should not a people seek unto their God? For the living to the dead?"

# SINS OF TEMPER

## HATRED

*I*t is malicious (the desire to harm others) and unjustifiable (wrong or unfair) feelings towards others, whether towards the innocent or by mutual animosity (bitter feelings). It is to feel extreme enmity (deep seated hatred) toward another. It is the same as murder.

1 John 3:15 "Whosoever hates his brother is a murderer; and you know that no murderer has no eternal life in him."

A biblical example of hate is in Genesis 37:4 "And when his brother's saw that their father loved him more than all his brethren, they hated him, and could not speak peaceably unto him."

Their hatred led to them getting rid of Joseph.

Genesis 37:28: "Then there passed by Midianites merchantmen; and they drew and lifted Joseph out of the pit, and sold him to the Ishmaelite for twenty pieces of silver; and they brought Joseph into Egypt."

Another example of hatred is racism. To hate a person or people because they may be a different race, color or have different religious beliefs is a form of hatred.

# VARIANCE

Variance is strife (bitter struggle between one another), contentions (forceful arguing), and enmity. God's people are not to promote controversies (between sides holding opposing views), disputes (arguing), or stupid, senseless arguments.

2 Timothy 2:23-26 "But foolish and unlearned questions avoid, knowing that they do gender strife. And the servant of the Lord must not strive; but be gentle unto all men, apt to teach, patient, in meekness instructing those that oppose themselves; if God peradventure will give them repentance to the acknowledging of the truth; and that they many recover themselves out of the snare of the devil, who are taken captive by him at his will."

# EMULATIONS

Emulations is to make war upon the good which is beheld in another, and thus to trouble that good and diminish it. It is also striving to equal or excel.

# WRATH

Wrath is a violent motion or passion of mind. It is an outburst of anger or a strong anger or indignation. We should not remain in wrath.

Ephesians 4:26 "Be angry, and sin not: let not the sun go down upon your wrath."

# STRIFE

Strife brings debates, contentions, factions, and disputes. We can devour one another in strife.

Galatians 2:6 "But from those who seemed to be something whatever they were, it makes no difference to me; God shows personal favoritism to no man for those who seemed to be something added nothing to me."

Galatians 4"26 "But the Jerusalem above is free; which is the mother of us all."

# SEDITIONS

Sedition is incitement to revolt against lawful authority. It causes division, a separate faction, and separation. In some cases, seditions can be done for the good of a people. For example the non-violent marches lead by Dr. Martin Luther King was for a purpose of justice for all mankind. We must be careful of the different faces of governmental groups being developed. Dr. King did not develop or establish a governmental group to be against the government. He taught ways and actions to fight for equality for all races.

The Apostle Paul was accused of being a mover of sedition among the people by the Pharisees. But he was preaching Christ and making a difference.

Acts 24:5 "For we have found this man a pestilent fellow, and a mover of sedition among all Jews throughout the world, and a ringleader of the sect of the Nazarenes."

# HERESIES

Heresy is a form of religious worship, discipline, opinion, or schism (an attempt to produce a split) that teaches contrary to the truth.

1 Corinthians 11:19 "For there must be also heresies among you, that they which are approved may be made manifest among you;"

# ENVYING

Envying is the feeling of displeasure produced by witnessing or hearing of the advantage or prosperity of others. Envy resents others success and hinders growth.

1 Peter 2:1-2 "Wherefore laying aside all malice, and all guile, and hypocrisies, and envies, and all evil speaking, as newborn babes, desire the sincere milk of the word, that you may grow thereby;"

# MURDERER

A murderer is those guilty of murder, unlawful slaughter, or slander. The world is full of murder. The media promotes it. We now have such easy means of carrying it out. Christians should not be involved in such.

1 Peter 4:15 "But let none of you suffer as a murderer, or as a thief, or as an evildoer, or as a busybody in other men's matters."

# SINS OF APPETITE

## REVELLINGS

Revel lings are feastings and drunkenness with impurity (immorality or sin) and obscurity (hidden acts) of the grossest (obscene, carnal, sensual) kind.

1 Peter 4:3 "For the time past of our life may suffice us to have wrought the will of the Gentiles, when we walked in lasciviousness, lusts, excess of wine, revellings, banqueting, and abominable idolatries;"

We are not to continue in those acts and ways.

## DRUNKENNESS

Drunkenness is habitual intoxication; the effect upon men of partaking of the abominations of the Babylonian's system.

Romans 13:13 "Let us walk honestly, as in the day; not in rioting and drunkenness, not in chambering and wantonness, not in strife and envying."

Revelations 17:2 "...and the inhabitants of the earth have been made drunk with the wine of her fornication.)

We are to stand faithfully as a Christian and deny the fleshly lust so that the Holy Spirit is in control. That will glorify God.

# LUST OF THE EYES

Be careful of what you fix your eyes upon continuously. Images in our mind can come from what we see. If it is allowed to replay repeatedly it will affect our thinking and eventually what we do.

Television is designed to influence our lives. There are programs for every facet of life.

The food channel makes eating delightful. If we cannot be temperate in our eating we need to stay away from that channel and all the food advertisements. Over eating affects our health. It does not provide for life and health.

The Bible says that man should not live by bread alone but by every word that proceeds out of the mouth of God. We make provision for over eating when we sit to watch television after dinner and see the commercials advertising food. Our flesh tells us to go and get some of what we see when we have already eaten. Gluttony is a sin.

The programs providing fashions and jewelry on television are another influence. We see it we want it. We don't need it we just want it. It is easy to order it from your home. What do we do to ourselves? We feed the flesh what it wants. We become so much in debt that we need two or three jobs. This takes our time from the things of God. We provide for our flesh by watching the programs and reading the magazines that entice us.

Sexual sins are also promoted by what we see. Sexual enticement is seen even in commercials and advertisements.

1 John 2:16 says, "For all that is in the world, the lust of the flesh, and the lust of the eyes, and the pride of life, is not of the Father, but of the world."

This applies to everything we can think of that is an image that we can see. There is nothing wrong with us eating food we like or having things we like. It becomes a problem when we cannot exercise temperance. Our inability to exercise temperance in all things can cause sickness, disease, and an abundance of financial debt.

We make it easy for the enemy (Satan) to hinder us when we do not feed the spirit man the word of God and it weakens. Our flesh becomes strong and those desires of the old man (the life before conversion) are awakened and begin to rule. Our old sinful nature was under the rule of Satan.

# THE PRIDE OF LIFE

*P*ride has a positive and negative side. We will deal with human pride, which is an antonym for humility. Pride is to be proud and exalted. It also denotes arrogance, evil behavior and perverse speech.

God blesses His people. He promised that we would be the head and not the tail, above and not beneath, the lender and not the borrower. As these promises are manifested in our lives we must remember God. God gives us favor. We can do nothing without God.

Israel, having been set apart by God, claimed its independence from God, and began to walk with an attitude of insolence.

Amos 6:8 says "The Lord God hath sworn by himself, saith the Lord the God of hosts, I abhor the Excellency of Jacob, and hate his palaces: therefore will I deliver up the city with all that is therein".

God hates pride even the way it looks. Pride is a conceited sense of one's superiority. When we walk in pride we become self righteous, we seek worldly power ambitiously. It hinders our progress and produces spiritual decay. Pride is one of the characteristics of men in perilous times.

2 Timothy 3:1-5 "This know also, that in the last days perilous times shall come. For men shall be lovers of their own selves, covetous, boasters, proud, blasphemers, disobedient to parents, unthankful, unholy, without natural affection, truce breakers, false accusers, incontinent, fierce, despisers of those that are good, traitors, heady, high-minded, lovers of pleasures more than lovers of God; having a form of godliness, but denying the power thereof; from such turn away."

We must remember that all unrighteousness is sin. Christ gave us his righteousness but he does not force us to walk in it. Our desire should be to walk in the righteousness of God continually. We do it by constant obedience to the Holy Spirit who leads and guides us in the word of God.

We are Christians. We are the called out ones by God. We are a chosen generation, a royal priesthood, and there is no area of living where we can be disobedient. We are to obey those that have rule over us in the secular and the spiritual. Where ever we go, work, school, home, and even medical obedience must prevail.

Once truth or instructions have been spoken to us, we are accountable for it. It hangs in the atmosphere over us. That is why God says He is faithful and just to forgive us our sins. When we are disobedient in any thing we need to ask for forgiveness.

We are dead to the power of sin, therefore sin should not reign in our mortal bodies. We can resurrect the power of sin over us by not continuing to walk in the spirit. As we live by the word of God, the fruit of the spirit grows in us and we begin to be more like Jesus Christ.

# CONCLUSION

*J*t is my prayer that the knowledge presented will bring an understanding of how we are making provisions for the flesh and giving place to the enemy. If we live our lives giving place to the enemy, and we are not aware that we are doing it, we will not live the abundant life God has for us. We will continue to live a life of struggles. And will not ask God for help. When we become aware of how we are giving place to the enemy, we will ask God to help us overcome. God's grace and mercy will abound in our lives.

If you are trying to reach a destination, and you are going the wrong direction, without the knowledge of going the wrong direction, you will move further from the destination. But once you realize you are going the wrong direction, you can turn and go the right direction and reach the destination.

Knowledge is power and we can make changes in the way we live.

Hosea 4:6 says the people perish for a lack of knowledge. If we know what is right, then do what is right, we will begin to live the abundant life that God has given.

Meditate on God's word; examine yourself to see what changes need to be made. Make the changes and walk therein. You will begin to see changes in your life that you thought were impossible. The blessings of God will follow you and overtake you. You will begin to walk like citizens of the kingdom of God. You will begin to look like people of the kingdom of God.

And what a witness of God our lives will become.

Made in United States
North Haven, CT
09 November 2023

43809079R00039